RISKS AND REWARDS

Ronald Stephenson
Risks and Rewards

Published by BooxAi

ISBN: 978-965-577-967-7

RISKS AND REWARDS

ONE MAN'S JOURNEY

RONALD STEPHENSON

Go placidly amid the noise and the haste, and remember what peace there may be in silence. As far as possible, without surrender, be on good terms with all persons.

Speak your truth quietly and clearly; and listen to others, even to the dull and the ignorant; they too have their story.

Avoid loud and aggressive persons; they are vexatious to the spirit. If you compare yourself with others, you may become vain or bitter, for always there will be greater and lesser persons than yourself.

Enjoy your achievements as well as your plans. Keep interested in your own career, however humble; it is a real possession in the changing fortunes of time.

Exercise caution in your business affairs, for the world is full of trickery. But let this not blind you to what virtue there is; many persons strive for high ideals, and everywhere life is full of heroism.

Be yourself. Especially do not feign affection. Neither be cynical about love; for in the face of all aridity and disenchantment, it is as perennial as the grass.

Take kindly the counsel of the years, gracefully surrendering the things of youth.

Nurture strength of spirit to shield you in sudden misfortune. But do not distress yourself with dark imaginings. Many fears are born of fatigue and loneliness.

Beyond a wholesome discipline, be gentle with yourself. You are a child of the universe no less than the trees and the stars; you have a right to be here.

And whether or not it is clear to you, no doubt the universe is unfolding as it should. Therefore be at peace with God, whatever you conceive Him to be. And whatever your labors and aspirations, in the noisy confusion of life, keep peace in your soul. With all its sham, drudgery and broken dreams, it is still a beautiful world. Be cheerful. Strive to be happy.

— 'DESIDERATA' BY MAX EHRMAN

* * *

An introduction is in order: First, this is not a self-help book, or a get-rich-quick essay. It is the story of one entrepreneur, his life, his failures, and successes. I have always believed that we all start out life on an equal footing, and everyone has the same opportunity to do what I have done. Of course, being born or finding yourself in America is a huge advantage. From the beginning, people have come to America to live out their dreams. It is the land of opportunity, and it is up to you to take advantage of what you have been given. There are about as many choices in life as there are people who make them. We live in a very new world, and all the old approaches to going about making a living have changed drastically. Once upon a time, you could get a job and if you wished, you could stay there until you dropped over or retired. Now, if the job lasts five years, that would make you an 'old timer'. Things are changing so rapidly that people find themselves in several jobs, and even then, they may be in totally different areas and require retraining or a lot of readjustment. For those who can adapt, this is an age where all the things you dream about are still possible. The internet has opened the entire world to you, and you can learn anything you set your mind to. It also offers countless opportunities to pick and choose how you would like to work. You no longer have to go some place, but can work from your home. To some, this can be overwhelming, representing a huge change in their life and routine. But for many, it leaves their future wide open.

Striking out on your own is not everyone's cup of tea. Everyone is not an independent thinker, and that is not a bad thing. So many people are easily contented with what life throws at them. Others will spend their life trying to find their place. Still, a few others seem to have a built-in plan on how they are going to do this thing called life. I can't stress enough about how we are all individuals, and it is up to each of us to choose our path, ignore the naysayers and get on with the adventure. It is important to never let someone try to run your life for you. When this happens, it is almost always doomed to failure.

It is a well-worn phrase, but a mind is a terrible thing to waste. I have lived long enough to meet and know a lot of unhappy people. It is sad to see folks with amazing potential that is literally thrown away. So often, people reach their fifties and realize that they have nothing to show for years of work, and have not saved anything for their retirement. Many were caught up in the idea of getting all the things they see others have, and waste their time, energy and money chasing things that won't make you happy. You only have so many years to get your life together, and the time you have flies by. It is tragic to see people give someone else twenty years of their life, or more, and still find themselves living paycheck to paycheck. For some, this is an unavoidable rut, and they accept it as normal. Others manage to escape the rat race and break out of this mindset.

For many, life is like a blueprint. You get an education, you get a job, you get married, you have children and work until you drop. You have obligations, and they can take priority over your life. You put all thought about eventual retirement out of your mind, and think things will go on forever. Then, you hit thirty-five or forty, and you have an epiphany. Big word for a big change in your thinking. Half your life is gone. Time for the big 'personal assessment'. And so it goes, and sometimes you have friends that broke the mold and went into business for themselves. Others go back to school and enter an entirely different field. There is something about them that strikes you as different. They seem to have a lot of confidence, and talk about all the things that are going on in their lives. And maybe, just maybe, you wonder how they pulled this all together. Maybe they were just born lucky, or they had a relative that gave them a business when they were ready to retire. They may have worked there for years, and when the owner decided to retire, he offered them the business. Lots of possibilities, and they are out there, just waiting for the right person to come along and 'seize' the opportunity. Is seize the right word? Yes; as opportunities pop up at the darnedest times. But you have to be ready, and that happened to me at least a half-dozen times.

Entrepreneur is French, and roughly translated, it means a risk taker. Gambling is a good example and a bad one at the same time. You are risking what you have with the idea that you are going to win. People in the gambling business know what they are doing; and you don't. They are not there to give away all the winnings, and you know that. But to some extent, we are all dreamers. When you borrow, it is much the same, as the person or institution is taking a chance on you paying them back, with interest. Again, a gamble. Would you put your house up as collateral to secure a loan to go into business? For most, this would be unthinkable. This is what separates the men from the boys, and the entrepreneur from the crowd.

At this point, you are probably asking yourself, 'why am I reading this?' I think you already know the answer. Somewhere in the back of your mind, this thought has come up. It is very easy to dismiss and for most, that is as far as it goes. Not to get sidetracked, as this is pretty heave stuff, but I have to tell you about a trip I took with one of my bankers to a neighboring town to look at still another business to buy. It was like my other two, and the man had built a substantial business that started out as a hobby. He was a college professor, and the business was taking too much away from what he loved to do, and that was teaching. He wanted to sell, but had no clear idea of what to ask for the business. This, believe it or not, happens frequently. There are many formulas to calculate the value of a business. The most common is gross annual sales. Others are more complex and call for goodwill, inventory, property, furniture and fixtures, lease obligations and the list goes on ad-infinitum.

My banker friend was dying to ask me a question. We talked all the time we were driving there. He wanted to know why and how I could even be thinking about still another business that would take a substantial investment. Without much thought, I told him this is what I do. I had worked for a number of people before going into business, and they were just jobs, and I knew how much money I was making them. They were no smarter than me, but somehow, I found myself working for them. Somehow, they had discovered the key to any business. As one person, you can only do so much, and that means you can only make so much. Of course, there are exceptions, but in the main you have to multiply your efforts to get ahead. And how do you do that? You hire people to work for you. In the case here, I would buy the business, keep most of the employees, maybe give them a raise, and just make a few adjustments in what was going on and grow the business. At this juncture, I owed about a million dollars in debt. My two other businesses were retail and you had inventory that was graciously lent to you, and a ten year lease on the properties from which you conducted your business. A side note: it is a genuine delight to use other people's money to run your business. I take some pride in saying that I paid everyone every dime I owed them, and that included some substantial interest in many cases.

Did I buy this business? No, as he could not be nailed down as to a price. I did all the standard calculations and presented them to him on more than one occasion. He just could not come to a number that would satisfy him and seem reasonable to me. You don't win them all. I have gone on to buy other businesses and have started a couple more from scratch. The point I am trying to drive home is that opportunities are out there, and few can see them unless you are looking for them. Businesses have a life span, just like people, and they come and go all the time. In the past couple years, we have seen the devastation caused by an epidemic with thousands of small businesses going under. That does not mean that the opportunities have gone away. Economies rise and fall, and there is always needs to be filled. There is a false assumption out there that says that if you have a business, you are rich and successful. Little do these laymen know what you have sacrificed to be your own boss, and what it takes to make a small business a success. The same can be said of what constitutes a fair profit. In my small business class, I asked my students what they thought a person made from their sales and services. Not surprisingly, many had no idea, and some wanted to say as much as doubling your money. In truth, you have to make at least one third, or you are not going to make it. That one third pays for inventory, wages, taxes, rent and utilities. In some cases, you need to budget for occasional advertising along with some gifts to charities for their fund-raisers. Often times, the owner takes no money from the business after he makes payroll. I often wonder how many ordinary wage-earning people could deal with that prospect? Sometimes, your reward is being your own person, and your success has come from being an independent operator and not someone else's employee. More often than not, it is not about the money.

For many, work is just another four-letter word, but if you enjoy what you are doing, you will never work another day in your life.

What if a person combined the events in their life along with the story of their successes and how they came about? I had read 'Hillbilly Elegy' a few months before, as it was a best seller and just got my curiosity going. Turns out, it was a true to life account of a person from the hills of Appalachia who came from nothing and made a name for himself. He is now a successful lawyer and is on television talk shows, is heavily involved in politics and may, at some point, run for office. He has been invited to numerous presentations and discusses poverty from first-hand experience. He graduated from Yale with a degree in law, to give you some further idea as to how far he has progressed. We all have more potential than we can imagine, but it is up to us to exploit it. It helps a bunch to get a good kick in the pants and a chance to meet people who know talent when they see it, encourage it and want you to succeed. It turns out that a movie was made of his story, and for those who are not ardent readers, you have a close to real life representation. It is important to note that not all people from that part of the world came up like this person. To be sure, there is a lot of poverty there, and it has taken its toll on many families, but there are others who have done well, like the life they have chosen and would not want to live anyplace else. Again, we are all individuals.

I am sure that many people have threatened to write a book at some point in their lives, and sometimes we are encouraged by others to do so. We put it off, and at best, we write our memoirs or something like that in a journal, thinking that at some point, we can sort it all out and it would be the makings of a best seller. Such are the daydreams of so many people. We all have a book in us, but we have to let it out. No one can help you with that.

Again, it is up to you. For those truly interested, there are hundreds of books out there on the subject of how to get started writing a book.

Such is the dream, and once in a while, it comes true. My life story is not a unique experience, and it has happened millions of times in America. It can be described as the American Dream, and it is now widely thought that it is just a dream. Happily, the American Dream is alive and well, and I, like so many others, am living proof that you can do the 'rags to riches' thing to this day. Success does not always translate into having or making a lot of money, but many folks tend to think that way. This is both a common misconception and the downfall of so many people. Money will buy freedom, independence and things, but it is still up to you to decide if you are going to be happy. In the end, it is all up to you, and how you go about finding fulfillment in your life is in the choices you make.

There is no one magic formula. You can research the success of others, and much has been written about so many people who have 'made it'. It has been estimated that about one person in a hundred will break out of their shell and go for the brass ring. Ah, there has to be a catch, right? Well, it is a little thing called 'risk', and few folks are capable of taking that step. By capable, I mean sacrificing what they have achieved in their lives and taking a gamble like starting their own business. Would you leave a steady, fairly good-paying job to follow some dream? Many have, and most fail. Why? Many reasons, but mostly it is the lack of research before they take the leap. You need to fully understand what you are getting yourself into, and the more you know, the better chance you are going to have to succeed. This risk thing is a big part of why most people are so hesitant to go into business for themselves. Yes, it takes money to make money. I am pretty sure that you have heard that phrase tossed around. It means you are going to risk what savings you have built up from working for someone else for half your life, or your parents or grandparents left you a little nest egg. If you own your own home, or have a mortgage, you may have some equity that you could put up to secure a loan. Borrowing money to start a business is one tough nut to crack, and banks and other investors will have to be convinced that you know what you are about to do and have put together a business plan that will prove that your idea is do-able. OK, say you find someone or some source that will loan you what you need to get started. You now have a partner who expects you to do your part. Any downsides to this grand plan? Actually, yes there is. You could lose everything in the process.

Oh, part two is thinking anyone you know will actually encourage you. For the most part, risk is a four-letter word, and even though they have never personally taken one this large, they will tell you all about the pitfalls and even throw in some horror stories to discourage you. You see, so many people do a basically good job of coping with their life, have made all the compromises, and any change is unknown territory. These are your family, your friends, the folks you work with every day. If you are really their friend and they trust you, they will readily admit that they do not like their job, but obligations, real and imagined, are holding them there. I have met and known so many people who are close to brilliant, but they cannot bring themselves to consider a major change in their lives. It may be an unhappy and untenable position, but it is what they have accepted for their lives. A sad state, but about eighty percent of people hate their jobs. If you have feelings of doubt welling up inside you, you may just want to run in the opposite direction. Small businesses have a failure rate of 90% in the first five years.

What does it take? Are you made up of the stuff it takes to make the leap? For starters, you need a good head start. Without a lot of help and advice at an early age, a fairly good education, and that little matter of 'research' I mentioned earlier, you cannot or should not take this journey. I won't bore you with too many details, but here is how it went for me, and I am fairly certain that you are an entirely different person, and your upbringing was entirely different. You may have had many more advantages and life was easy. If you were handed a good education and got into a career path that matched your training. For some, this works out, while others realize that they are not cut out for what was chosen; by them or by others. This isn't the end of the world, and life is a continuing adventure; if you want it to be.

The story begins with my origins. I am the eighth living child of my aging parents. At 42, my mother had her last and tenth child. I was welcomed into the world by two parents and seven siblings; five sisters and two brothers. So far, nothing unusual, right? With the help of my family,

I was shown early how to read and write, to sing and remember lyrics to songs. I was spoiled. My siblings taught me basic math, and when the books came home from school, I was right there to watch and listen. When you are very young, you are like a sponge and can readily absorb most everything placed in front of you. Now, on the surface, you would think this was a big advantage. But it takes a lot more than that. You need to be encouraged to learn and, most of all, to think. Some of us were in the right place at the right time and things fell into place early on. We had parents and family and teachers to pique our interest. We had older people who delighted in telling us about their lives and what they did. Never forget that everyone has a story, and there is wisdom to be found in learning early to be a good listener.

Starting school was very difficult for me. I was sheltered for those first six years and the thought of being separated from my family was too much to bear. I cried a lot, but things got better with time. I soon got the hang of it, and my siblings were in the same school, so it wasn't complete isolation. Learning came easy to me. While others were learning to read and write, I had that under my belt, so the world of learning was wide open. You can just guess how I was treated by my teachers. I went through the work books like it was just an exercise, yet they were designed for a semester. The teachers challenged me, and I did my best not to disappoint them. Life was good and I hoped this would never end. When we are young, we live in the moment, and it is wonderful.

Ok, what was it like to be poor? It really depends upon the person, and in my case, there was lots of love with two older parents, being the baby of the family and brothers and sisters close at hand to teach me what they already knew. What an advantage! Then, at the age of five or six, our lives changed for the worse. My father was a meatcutter, worked for a very large meatpacking firm in the St. Louis area. We were living the working class life. We lived in a nice home in the suburbs, with a large yard and a garden and lots of flowers to be smelled and sampled. We had a garden, and my father enjoyed growing things, I followed him around, and during the planting season, he put me to work as a potato planter. He had cut potatoes into quarters after they had sprouted 'eyes', and these were placed in the ground at a desired depth with the eyes facing up. I was four years old at the time. I need to mention that we had a fairly large crop for a home garden, and much more than we could use. He made a practice of giving them to neighbors who may have really needed a little help. I bring this up to point out that your upbringing has a profound impact on your life. As you will see, much of what I learned about sharing at an early age carried over into the jobs and careers later in my life. Then it happened. My father collapsed at work, and it was learned that the forty-two degree work environment had damaged his health. Doctors advised that he needed to work outdoors with moderate temperatures and fresh air. Economically, this was the beginning of some hard times. We lost that little piece of heaven and moved back toward town and wound up in a small duplex, next to railroad tracks, with an outhouse for a bathroom. We had a chicken coop in the back yard, and many meals consisted of chicken. At my age, I could not really understand what had happened, and it had next to no impact on my life. I took it all in, and it was the first of many adventures in my life. Across that large series of railroad tracks was the largest park in the town, and it had a lagoon, and gardens, and what seemed like miles of open spaces. At that time the second Great War was already in progress. My oldest brother was drafted and that meant a further loss of income to our family. With the help of one of my sisters, we were able to stay in our humble rented home. My father kept finding jobs, but none of them lasted, so it was a difficult time. My schooling was about to start, and I don't think that system offered Kindergarten, so I was six when my formal education started. More change was right around the corner, and that involved a move to northern Indiana where there were jobs aplenty for the likes of my father. He had a very good skill set for an uneducated person. He and his brother built houses for a living, and he could fix just about anything.

Then the first of many moves took place in my life. It was to become a standard procedure in the Stephenson household. We moved from Southern Illinois to Northern Indiana, and that meant a new home and a new school. The small refinery town of Whiting, Indiana was to be my home town for all my primary and secondary school years. My father's health had failed while we lived in East St. Louis, and he was now advised to seek outdoor work, as his meat-cutting job of many years had taken its toll, and he collapsed at his work station. That was the reason for the move and it was perhaps one of the best things that could have happened to my family and me. My oldest sister, Louise, lived in that town with her husband, Fred, and we just moved in with them. Back then, that was not an unusual circumstance. We lived with them until my father landed a job and found a place for us to live. My father's health improved, and he found a job in the construction industry. Our income shot up and we prospered in comparison to what we had before. The town was a favorite of the John D. Rockefeller Foundation, the founder of the Standard Oil Company, and the town benefited in so many ways due to their generosity. We had a huge community center and some excellent schools due to the large tax base the refineries provided. Whiting was what is commonly called a factory town, and the refinery was the major employer. The huge steel mills were close by, and jobs were plentiful.

That all worked in my favor, and it was paradise to go to school, make new friends and use the beautiful Carnegie library most any time. I spent a good part of my summers at the library and got interested in all manner of subjects. I loved the natural sciences and devoured book after book in that area. I liked school so much that I convinced myself that my main ambition in life was to become a school teacher. More on that later. There was the discovery that I had artistic talent too, and that was encouraged by the art teacher who was employed by the school system. I studied and practiced oil painting, water color, sculpture and the rest. By my junior and senior year I was helping with the seventh and eighth grade art classes. I was elected to become the president of the school's art club. In another instance, I was elected to presidency of the biology club. I missed the point of being in the National Honor Society by one teacher vote.

So, when did the 'itch' come upon me to try my hand at free enterprise? I was twelve years old, and comic books were what young people read. In the back, there was usually some ads for things kids like, along with opportunities to make some money. Even at that age, I was ready to jump in and see what this was all about. The item to sell was glow in the dark shade pulls, and a few other items made out of the same stuff. All you had to do was canvass the neighborhood and show off these trinkets and take orders. At twelve, you are some sort of 'model kid' with ambition, and it was so easy to do, as people would encourage ambition back then. It was a success, and after everyone was solicited in my neighborhood, that adventure was over. I made a few dollars, and that bought a few things a kid wants, like extra candy and more comic books. At that point, I had been bitten. It wasn't until the next summer that another opportunity came up. My friend and his family were going on vacation, and like me, he had a summer job riding a three-wheeled contraption made out of a bicycle on three wheels and a refrigerated box on the front to hold ice cream. You pedaled around the neighborhoods and rang some bells, and kids and adults would come running to buy a cold treat. For me, it was like a license to make money, and those were some profitable weeks. At fourteen, I applied and received a work permit from the school system. My grades were such that it was not difficult to convince them that I would not neglect my studies. Yes, I was an A student. That carried on throughout my school years. My classmates were largely second generation Eastern Europeans. That is not to say anything derogatory about them. This was a refinery town, and people from all over this country and Europe came to America for good jobs and the life that it would support. There was some friction in having to deal with hillbillies like my brother and me. He too was an excellent student and well-liked by the faculty. Being scarcely three years apart, we had mutual interests and common friends. We liked English, math, science, electronics and the natural sciences. We gravitated toward older, educated people and found them to be an important part of what would be our adult lives. Our teachers were some of the best this well funded system could attract. Many had masters degrees in their area of teaching.

Those years were to be some of the best ones in my life, and my guess is that many people think the same way. My first real job came at fourteen, and it was washing windows and sweeping up in a local shoe store. I was promoted to salesperson at about the same time, and that meant more income. By this time, I was helping the family, as my father was in a field that did not provide a steady income. It is said that hard work pays off, and in my case, it was just the beginning. I liked the idea of working and being rewarded for doing so. This is perhaps a big part of the building blocks it takes to 'get ahead' in this world.

High school flew by. In a wink I was graduated and off to full-time work. I remained in the shoe business, working many hours and making a decent living for a young, single person. I had cars and clothes, spending money and quite a few friends. I had two offers for college scholarships and turned them down. I was your typical home boy, and never dreamed of leaving my home community and all my friends and family. That turned out to be one of the first major mistakes in my young life. I truly regret not taking up the offers for scholarships, but I was on a management track, and the doors were starting to open. I would have my own retail store to manage, and at 21, that was a big opportunity. Realize this was in the fifties, and back then, you were rated by merit more than 'credentials'. That was actually a standard back then, and a high school education would have been comparable to a four year degree now. Degrees were needed in the education system back then, and few people pursued a degree except for the professions. The GI bill kicked in after the Second World War, and veterans were encouraged to take advantage of this new benefit. That was the point in America when higher education took off. Now, four years of sitting on your bottom will get you a degree in most anything and may get you a ticket to apply for jobs requiring that piece of paper. It is ironic in a way, that a person like myself would find me interviewing for jobs requiring a degree, and getting the jobs every time. To this day, I believe that a degree will get you the interview, but not necessarily a job. You are your own best salesperson. You have to display confidence and ambition.

My days were numbered, and I was aware of the fact that the military draft was still in effect, and any male turning age eighteen had to register. You merely went to the nearest post office and filled out a simple form. For all of us, that was a ticking time bomb in our lives. Of course, many of my classmates volunteered and went into the service. Your 'out' was to get married and have a family started. In fact, two of my friends opted for that route, and I am sure many men took that option. Then the sky fell in. Just after I turned twenty three, I was drafted. They gave me thirty days to get my affairs in order. The next two years are what I call the 'growing up' phase of my life. I quickly found out that the real world was a very large place, and it was time to adapt and fit in. Again, good fortune came knocking. Barely into basic training, I was scooped up and offered an opportunity to join the Army Intelligence Corps and was sent to Fort Holabird in Baltimore, Maryland to learn the job of military intelligence coordinator after fourteen weeks of intensive classroom study. This does not ordinarily happen for people drafted for two years. Apparently, my test scores were sufficiently high to get screened out, or is that 'in'? Then there was the security clearance which started with an extensive background investigation by several federal agencies tasked with that job. I was to learn later that about half my small town was questioned. The learning started all over again. I even looked into taking some college courses. The University of Maryland had a strong interest in the military and the educational opportunities it could offer those in military service. I went so far as to take the entry exams to see if I was college material. To my surprise, I was informed that I had reached a three and a half year college level rating. My guess was it was sufficient knowledge to continue on with my life, with or without a college degree. This time it was to learn all about how the army operates from the ground up. I had no idea of how things worked, even though I had relatives and friends who served in wartime. One of the cruel jokes in the military is they offer you a chance to specify where you would like to be assigned when you finish your training. My choice was to get as close to where I grew up as possible and that was the Chicago area. You had to pick three preferences, so my next choice would have been Germany or Panama. That never happened. Having been trained in Baltimore, Maryland at Fort Holabird, it was not to be. I met with the sergeant who made the decisions on where we were to be sent. I tried to point out my preferences on the forms and he gave me a strange look. He then explained one of the most common answers in the military; the needs of the service outweigh everything else. He pointed to a vacant desk, about three desks behind him, and told me that was where I was to spend the rest of my two years. He had looked at the scores on my form and realized I was a decent typist, and that is what he needed. So I began my service time working in an office, five days a week. I was given a lot of responsibility in a short amount of time. I was assigned to personnel and records, and that spilled over into personnel management at a fairly high level. It was a far cry from the training I had received, but you are given what the Army says they need, and not necessarily what you would like to do or have been trained to do. I want to point out that our government at that time was in to what we now call the Cold War, and those of us currently in the service were extended indefinitely. It was the time of the Cuban Crisis, and we watched then President Kennedy tell us what was going on. So, instead of the original two years of service, I could have remained a few more months or years until the crisis was over. My job changed rapidly, as my real assignment was managing the records of the intelligence corps personnel and they were leaving for Florida by the day. Much processing on not very much time. We lost about half of the people assigned to us. Once the crisis was over, we were back to normal tour of duty status, and the extension was just part of our days served. Things reverted back to normal in a couple months, and my calendar was getting shorter by the day.

Upon learning that I had artistic skills, the various divisions asked me to draw up organization charts for each of them, and that freed me from my regular duties for a time. It also exposed me to how the army is organized and later I realized that their operational methods spill over into civilian life, and most major corporations had adopted military structures in their business. Responsibility seemed to follow me around, and I was assigned the task of bay sergeant for my group of twenty-four men, and had the task of keeping them in line and doling out the work details. It was a short two years, and I had grown up a lot. I was offered Officer Candidate School, but turned that down. I wanted out and back to civilian life. I came away with more confidence and learned a lot about myself and what my capabilities were. I made a number of friends in the time spent, stood up for a wedding for one couple, and we stayed in touch for years afterward. The military will make a man out of a boy in a short amount of time. Those with no direction in their young lives would do well to join the military and discover what their life can be with some purpose in it.

Back to civilian life was a big letdown. Three months back in the grind, and It quickly became obvious that this was just a dead-end job with no real future. My boss was now in his fifties and was resigned to finishing his life up to retirement as a store manager. For those not familiar with retail sales, the hours were horrendous. You worked from nine AM to 9 PM six days a week. You worked, you partied, and you slept. That was your life and as an assistant manager, it meant opening and closing the place each night. Right there and then, I decided that was not the way I was going to wind up. I told him that I was not going to pursue a management position in their chain of stores. He shot back with that was all I knew how to do. That turned out to be the proverbial last straw. A few days passed, and I decided to take a look at what was out there. This was 1963, and the economy was booming, and it was easy to walk across the street to a new job. Right down the street was an employment agency. These days, we call them headhunters, but it was the right move. My first interview got me the job and I was off to a selling job at more money and a lot more time off. My new title was Account Executive, and it was a credit and collection firm with ties to the Chamber of Commerce and the Credit Bureau. My job was simple enough. It required me to convince people to give their bad accounts to my firm, where we would try to collect the amounts owed for a percentage. It was fun and exciting, and the money was good for that time period. I was good at convincing people to trust us with their bad accounts, and had a great opportunity to land one of the largest accounts in the county. The utility company offered both gas and electricity, and as such, they were the go-to for utilities. Like most large corporations, they did very well, and with no competition, they had little interest in the losses they got from non-paying customers. Everyone in the firm, including the owner, had tried to convince these folks to give us their business. As they say, the field was wide open, and I decided to pursue the account. I found my way into the treasurer's office through persistence, and it paid off. The man was curious as to why someone my age would try to convince him that we could work to solve a long-standing problem of uncollectible debts. He confided in me that the managers of the local offices were responsible for this issue, but there was a natural reluctance to try to collect bad debts. After a number of visits, he finally decided to give us a try, and called one of the branches and instructed them to give us the old, bad accounts for a trial period. This was a breakthrough in the collection business in our county, as we had competition and everyone had tried to crack this account. It turned out to be a windfall, and we were given all the old utility bills for years past. We had a close relationship to the Chamber of Commerce and the credit bureau that they also ran. If someone owed a utility bill, it would be difficult to get service, so we had a lot of leverage in that regard. The money poured in, and my hope was that this would mean a promotion or at least a substantial raise. As I recall, the owner gave me a fifty dollar bonus and maybe a fifty dollar a month raise. Talk about being disappointed. I had risked my steady job to take on this new challenge, and in two years' time, I was locked in to still another job with no real future. It was a small business and the owner was not about to take his youngest employee and promote him. His staff had been with him for years and ran the three offices they had in the different cities. Now, at that time, this was a good job, with good pay and only five days a week. Compare that to six days and twelve hours a day in the shoe business. At twenty-five, I was single, living at home, was driving a new Jaguar XK-E, and had my other hobby cars to play with. As they say, life was good.

All went well for that two year period, and I married in 1964 to a wonderful woman I had dated for five years. I was fortunate to have someone who supported me and encouraged me to move on. We had four boys in just five years, so we were finished with child-making and concentrated on making a good living to support our offspring. My boss of those two years decided that I could do even more for him if he spent a little money on training. He enrolled me in the Dale Carnegie courses in public speaking and human relations. This course is offered to this day, and is a requirement in many industries and businesses for those on an upward career path. It is an intense program to bring people out of their 'safe zone' and teach them assertiveness and self confidence. Again, an opportunity to grow, to gain more confidence and to seek even more opportunities. The main advice from this group was to get out there and use the skills I had gained by volunteering to speak and make presentations for a charity. I think they put it like 'use it or lose it'. This started the ball rolling, and the American Cancer Society became the focus of still more learning and experience. I became the spokesperson for many of their presentations on cancer prevention. There was a big push back then to discourage smoking, and that was a favorite for men's clubs. As for women's organizations, I had to give presentations on Breast Cancer self examinations and cervical cancer screenings. I know what you are thinking, and it was all 'educational' with pamphlets. And very little in the question and answer periods. After many presentations over a period of a few months, they approached me with a job offer. It caught me by surprise, as I truly thought that the whole operation was voluntary. They offered more money and quite a benefit package to go with it. Accepting it meant telling my current employer of my intentions of leaving his firm. I wrote a 30 day notice of resignation and handed it in. That did not go well, and began a month of discussions and lunches to try to convince me to stay. He was very disappointed and told me that he had never lost an employee. First, they could not match the pay and benefits, and promises are not negotiable items, so I held my ground and followed through on leaving. Within six months, he made an effort to rehire me and had no success. I was on my way in an entirely new field. All that outside exposure in every major city in that county was a real plus. I had contacts and knew the collection clients quite well, as part of my job was to call on them from time to time to pick up accounts.

Being in the employ of the American Cancer Society was more than making speeches to clubs and other organizations. My new title was Campaign Director and that meant being in charge of their annual campaign for funds. Their term for the fundraiser was Crusade for a cure. My boss, a retired nurse, had been looking for someone to replace the man who did this job. He had moved on in the organization to a much higher position, leaving her high and dry. The next step was my continuing education; this time in fund raising and community organization.

I was sent to their national training seminar for two weeks of intense training. It was in Kansas City and was like a summer vacation to me. The fundraising aspect really got my attention, and all that I learned was put to the test, with a lot of success. We were the second highest campaign in Indiana, next to Indianapolis, and that registered in several quarters, as we were not in the United Way and we did this right under their noses in the city of Gary, Indiana. Two successful campaigns and the political winds shifted, and I became a victim of the 'restructuring'. After spending considerable money training me, I was sure I would eventually be running my own chapter as a director. That was not to be, but the United Way of Gary had had their eye on me all along, and approached me to consider working for them as their campaign director. As I recall, I was out of a job for about two weeks before my life changed once again! Again, more money, great benefits and still more responsibility. This time we were shooting for that magic one million dollar campaign that eluded them for years. My work for the Cancer Society gave me access to hundreds of volunteers that I had recruited for them, and it was an easy matter to draft these people for the new adventure.

Success brought recognition, and I was soon on my way for some more training at the National Headquarters of United Way of America in Alexandria, Virginia. Two weeks of orientation in their approach to fundraising and administration. I came away from that experience with even more confidence and went on to seek even bigger goals for myself and my current employer. Then the door opened once again. It seems that all the twelve United Ways in that huge metropolitan area of Northwest Indiana were negotiating to merge. Our Gary facility was the largest in the county, and we were the top choice for control of all the funds, along with a neighboring community who also was in the running. We finally negotiated a merger with the second-largest fund to ours, and I remained the campaign director for two of the larger communities. The other big holdout community, Hammond, Indiana, was not very enthusiastic about joining, but eventually, they joined the fold. I now had three combined campaign responsibilities and had an office, a paid staff and three bosses. It is best to have one boss, but to have three, and all of them vying for the top job, as they were all still employed by the three major funds in the package. When the dust settled, the first merger's director won the job, and he was now my only boss. He was an excellent manager and we hit it off immediately. His background was in public relations, and he had a degree in that field. He had worked for the now-defunct Studebaker/Packard Corporation in South Bend, Indiana. While there, he worked as a volunteer for the local United Way and was offered a job when his parent company closed. He then moved to East Chicago, Indiana as that fund's executive director. Now he was in charge of the whole merger, and we began to reach out of the industrialized area and attempt to bring in the other smaller communities. My fundraising duties expanded into offering our help in their fund drives, and they were all quite receptive to the idea of having professional staff help them with the annual campaigns.

My experience with the county-wide Cancer drives came in handy, as I had contacts in all of the remaining communities in the county. With good success, it was an easy matter to bring them into the fold. We were now the Lake Area United Way and the money really started rolling in. We reached over six million dollars in our first combined attempt, a record that stands to this day and has never been repeated. The next chapter was about to begin, and I was not prepared for it. My boss had decided that I needed to move on, and he had been grooming me to take on my own directorship in another community. He had been pushing me with the national organization and I found myself being invited to chair the small communities sessions at the annual conference. He also pushed me to get involved with the State of Indiana United Way and I came on that board as a representative. While there, I met with most of the directors of the other United Ways. My boss was nearing retirement, and he wanted me to move ahead, and I then realized he was treating me like his own son.

And then it came. A very short meeting, and I was out the door with a severance package and a great letter of recommendation. Now what? Next thing was to inform my wife of the situation, and that we might have to move away in order for me to get my own directorship. Not a good experience. We had both lived in that community all our lives, and the thought of moving was a very difficult idea to wrap our heads around. We had lots of friends and many activities that we were happy with and contented with our lives. And our families were all close by, so that made it all the harder. On top of that, we had just gotten our new home in a new area. I had taken part in designing it to fit our needs with a growing family, and when all this happened, we were settled in and planned to spend a good many years in our new home. The alternative was to try and find local employment that would pay as well and provide all the benefits a young family needed. One of our friends was a contractor, and he worked with a development firm who built and sold houses. I knew him well and we were friends, so I told him what had happened. He suggested that I contact the company he worked for about a position in sales. After a lengthy interview, it was mutually decided that I would not fit in to this company's plans. He wanted someone who would not leave him if something else came up, and I was honest and told him my situation. I don't recall if I ever tried to find something else locally, although I would have taken something in my field or in sales that would pay as well to support my family. It would not be long before the severance money ran out, and I had to do something soon.

I began immediately to put together a convincing resume and contacted the national organization's human resources group. I gathered up recommendations from community leaders who knew me and worked with me on the campaigns. All this went to the national organization and the search began. In a month's time, a position came up in Terre Haute, Indiana, about three hours down the road from where we were living. I was invited to come and interview, and things went quite well. The local fund was the problem. It was fraught with problems with fund raising and agency dissatisfaction. The director of five years there could not raise the money necessary to increase the budgets of the agencies. I knew the director from meetings at the state level and he seemed to be a nice sort, but did not have the fire in the belly to raise money and run a United Way. Things were stagnant and a lot of change was needed. My resume caught their eye as a community organizer and a successful track record in fund raising. The job interview was with the executive committee of the board, and the president was also the President of Indiana State University. He listened to the others for some time. There were lots of questions, and then it came. He wanted to know if I had ever taught. I was on my toes, and looked at him calmly and answered 'just adults'. Almost immediately, I was offered the job and a substantial pay raise, plus their willingness to pay for my move. Breaking the news to my wife was not a happy circumstance and she was very resistant at first. But once she realized it was going to happen, she could do two things: one, she could stay there and I could come home on weekends, or she could accept the idea and come down to the new community and help me find a house. My oldest was just starting school, and we were fairly certain that a move would not harm him that much. The rest of the brood was young and had not established that many friends.

Getting established and settling in a new community is not an easy task. It would be months before I could move my family to a new home, and the task before me was to find a house to rent, then start the search for a new, permanent home. It is like being pulled in two directions at once, as most of my time was being devoted to a huge problem of reorganizing a community fund drive. House hunting can best be described as being sporadic, and the community was much smaller, narrowing down the field of choices. My wife came down on weekends, and we looked at a number of homes that were for sale. None seemed to fill all the blanks, as we had just built a new house and had settled in to exactly what we wanted. The idea of building new once again became an option, and there were new developments taking place in an other-wise stagnant market. We landed on what seemed to be the perfect spot for a new house, and the developer was young and starting out in the business. It was a good match, and we agreed to start the process. We actually got much more than we expected and we had a new 'dream home' built. Imagine a couple in their mid-thirties getting a home that people in their fifties would build after the kids were gone? How about an English Tudor, two stories high on a waterfront lot in a very private subdivision? Things were looking up. It turned out that the contractor had under-estimated what it would cost to build, and offered us ten thousand more than we agreed to buy the house he was building for us.

And so, a new chapter for me and my family was about to unfold. Moving into a new and strange community is not an easy task, and you have to quickly establish contact with community leadership and familiarize yourself with how things work and who calls the shots. The quicker this is accomplished the easier job it is to make the transition. This board had a good mix of the community and the large local college, and they were all frustrated with what was going on. No one appeared to take the point position, and they were looking for guidance. I was a good twenty years younger than the youngest person on the board, so it was going to be hard to get points across in too hasty a fashion. I decided to take it slow and enjoy the 'honeymoon' while it lasted. The first order of business was to target in on the fundraising campaign, and some of that was already decided, but there was a long way to go, and the locals did not have any training in the way to go about putting on a successful campaign. That sounds like a harsh assessment, but I had been through that before in a much larger community. I put together a training presentation, and everyone involved, including the board, got the message. I had received a lot of help from the national organization in my training with them, and it went together quickly. Now to meet the thirty member agencies.

This was one very unhappy bunch. No increases for years and arguments over what they could and could not do to raise needed funds created a lot of friction, and many had threatened to leave the fold and go out on their own. This is bad for the organization, and communities are torn apart when this happens. The challenge was to meet with them as a group and try to calm the waters; to ask for some time to make things right. Most social agencies are not equipped to do fund raising beyond a membership drive, and most are staffed with social workers as directors. Now, before you assume I look down on social workers, you need to understand that management and bookkeeping is not a part of their training, and many could not balance their own checkbook, let alone manage the budget in their organizations.

Welcome to my new office! That is being extremely charitable. We were housed in what used to be the shower and locker room for a local plant, and the floors were slanted inward to allow the water to drain. The heating and air conditioning units were as old as the building, and were maintained by the company owners. Our agency and two others used this space, and it was politely called 'crowded'. My 'staff' consisted of a bookkeeper and a secretary/receptionist. As expected, they were not highly paid, and it showed, but that was the mentality of this community when it came to 'charities'. It was uncomfortable at first, as the former director was reluctant to move, even though he had been dismissed. He would come in as though nothing had happened. I knew him from my association with other directors in Indiana, and it was difficult for him to accept the fact that I was going to take over his job. After about a month, he stopped coming in, and apparently found a job locally with a printing company. He had put down roots in the community and decided to leave the United Way field. This is not unusual in the social work field, and I have seen it occur many times. People coming out of school with a social work degree look forward to getting a position in a not for profit organization and working with people in need. I have known people who lasted two years and just became overwhelmed with the problems their clients endure, and limited resources available to help them. The caseload is typically way more than any one person can handle, and burnout is common.

Our giving records, the life blood of this type of organization, were outdated and the system itself was old school. Far from the sophistication that we had in a well-funded organization, it needed a shot in the arm; more like a massive I-V. I had to approach the board and ask for more budget. They had hung on to what was the precursor, the local Community Chest, and it held on to reserved funds, trusts and legacies. That was the vehicle we needed to approach. I put together a presentation, went over it with the officers of the board, and we approached that board with our needs. They agreed to a one-year grant to expand our staff and fund the campaign to raise more money. Without the injection, we would have remained dead in the water. You can make bricks without straw, but it is a lot harder.

Expansion time. I needed help, and I had someone in the wings that I had worked with in the other funds. Jack came on board, and we were a team once again. He would handle some of the staffing of the campaign and I could spend more time organizing and playing the agency diplomat. His forte was in public relations and publicity. He could put our story out to the public through the local media. I had added a third office person and gave the staff a raise. A raise is the world's greatest motivator, and it had that exact effect.

Things began to turn around, and the organization was coming together quickly. The agencies were asked to join in the campaign, to make calls and go into stores, offices and factories and tell them about the services they provided in the community. For some unknown reason, it seems that this idea had never taken root in this community, and likely was part of the 'separation' between the United Way and the agencies. The volunteers on the boards got active in the campaign, and they represented the leadership in the community. It was a natural marriage and things really started rolling.

Like most United Ways, this one had a labor participation committee, and as best I can describe, they were not liked by most of the board. Terre Haute is a union town, and without their cooperation, you could not do effective employee solicitation at worksites. I had come from a huge labor-intensive situation in my previous position, and it was very easy to find the necessary cooperation with the union leaders. They checked me out with the community I left to satisfy themselves that I was 'cooperative'. We had a labor staff representative on the payroll, but they were not included in much of the affairs of the fund. That changed immediately, and I suddenly found myself with an enthusiastic third professional staff person. She was a union leader in the telephone industry and was very good at working with people. She had retired after many years and had kept her activities going with the Central Labor Union.

The first three years were hectic, as much had to be done to convince the powers that be; the board, that we needed to step into the future, embrace the concepts of a true United Way, and expand our efforts in the community to encourage a wider acceptance of our programs and that of the agencies we served. It took a lot of convincing and many orientation meetings, but it came to fruition and we were on our way. We raised more money almost immediately, and things were looking up. My continued relationship with the National organization continued, and I was invited to join the national conference committee and head the small business division of the conference. Things were looking good, and my expectation of moving forward was always in the back of my mind. I now regret getting comfortable in the job, and stayed on beyond my welcome. Eight years had passed, and we were just coasting with no new increases in income. Not a good sign and pretty discouraging to be part of a stagnating organization. I have to confess that boredom had set in, and my enthusiasm was waning for the job. It was at that time that I just knew that things might change for the worse, as everything that needed to be done had been completed. One day, my feet propped up on my desk, and my thoughts were about my future and where to go from here. If I stayed in the United Way movement, I would have to move again to a new community, and in doing so, would I be happy doing essentially the same thing until I retired? That was probably the shortest question and answer session I had ever experienced. My hobbies kept me interested in outside activities, and our social life was going fine, as we had established ourselves in the community. I had an 'itch' that could not be scratched, and it turned out to be the beginning of a new chapter in our lives. I learned that I had board members who had the same thoughts, and I learned that even some members had designs on my job, and it was only a matter of time before this became obvious to everyone involved.

Then, a funny thing happened in the middle of my life, and it is called the midlife crisis. It comes upon you and suddenly you realize that half your life could be over and you try to put all the pieces in place and make some sort of assessment as to how far you have come and what the future might look like. I was 38 or 40, and this was like a lightning bolt. I was in bed after a long day, and this came up on me out of the blue. It happens to most men, and it can be likened somewhat to menopause in women, but I am sure it is not the same thing at all. Regardless, it happens, and it is the eye-opener of your life. It becomes a time to assess what you have done, and what the future might look like. It could be a time to let things flow, a time to coast and let things happen on their own, or take charge of your life and start getting busy with what future you have left. So; what David Thoreau said was true, and it is a fact that 'the mass of men lead lives of quiet desperation'. We just don't realize it until we get a wake-up call that rings our bell. It may be wonderful if this did not happen, but it is there and we are not given any warning or 'advance notice'. I have often wondered why this isn't taught in schools.

My new found 'coasting period' led to changes that turned out to be beneficial. One of my hobbies was home electronics, and I had friends who shared the interest. Some actually worked in the business and it was a very hot market at the time, as everyone who could afford it wanted a home stereo system. It turned out that there was a growing market for used equipment, and a friend and I dabbled in that market with some success. The friend made his living selling the equipment and wanted to do something more with his knowledge. The idea of opening a store came up, and the more we discussed it, the more appealing the idea became. There were two or three stores in our town that dealt in home entertainment, and the friend worked for two of them at one time. Then it happened; as one of the better stores came up for sale. We moved quickly and made an offer. The problem; financing, but even that worked out, as the friend's father was willing to invest in his son's future. We suddenly found ourselves in the audio business and things began to really take off. At the time, I was still the director of the United Way, and it became a juggling act to keep both the candle ends burning. It became obvious to the board that something had to be done. That was the beginning of the end of my United Way career. By 1983, it was over, and I found myself president of a company I had started in the retail field. Things just took off from there. Sales increased dramatically, and we had to hire more staff to keep up with customer demands. I even looked at stores in neighboring communities as a part of possible expansion. The first three years was a honeymoon of sorts, and I found a new sense of freedom and independence. Gone were the constant demands of management, board meetings, committee meetings, fund raising and agency relations. Oh, I don't want to leave out the politics that goes with organizations like United Ways. It was intoxicating! I had free time and extra money to spend on things like collector cars. Owning and running a small business is an adventure that few will experience in their lifetimes. You are chief bottlewasher, manager, bookkeeper and your own boss. Things were going great, and we were growing very quickly. We added staff and expanded our lines. As luck would have it, things began to change, and our relationship deteriorated to the point where we began to avoid each other. His father had hoped that being in a job that could not fire his son was the answer to a life-long problem of parenting. My partner could not hold down a job, and his adult life required assistance on an almost constant basis from the parents. Their last, best hope was to make a man of him, and also a self-sufficient manager of a business. I tried everything I could think of to bring him into the fold of eventually becoming the manager, and had many discussions with his father on what progress we had made. My partner was very intelligent, but lacked focus and could not concentrate on grasping the concept of decision making. I became more than just frustrated and could see the writing on the wall. Something had to be done, or I would be strapped with a dependency role, with less and less freedom to act on my own behalf. Time to jump ship. Imagine throwing away an opportunity like this. I tried to buy them out, but the father would have no part of it. He was in his seventies and had spent his life trying to make a man of his son. On the personal side, the part owner was a friend for at least five years. We had many great times together. That relationship dissolved when I informed him that I was leaving. I did not realize what a dependency I had built up in him. We grew distant and hardly communicated after that. Things deteriorated rapidly but it did not affect the business itself. We were making money right and left, and the business continued for a few more years after we parted ways. Another factor at this point was the bottom was beginning to fall out of the stereo business. It was perhaps a bitter time for me with the loss of a friendship and a profitable business.

An interesting development came into play at the closing of this relationship, as still another employee had similar ideas of opening a business in the same line of home entertainment. He and his brother were experienced sales people, primarily in the jewelry business, and were excellent salesmen. With my credit and reputation in the business, we could start a business from scratch and compete with my former partners. Not exactly a revenge arrangement, but to carry on with another highly profitable business. I call this period the Audio Wars era, and it brought on some fierce confrontations. Once again, I had gotten myself into an 'arm's length' arrangement with my new partners. I would cover the start up and they would run the store. On the surface, a smashing success, but little did I know that our goals were not shared. They saw it as a golden opportunity to make lot of money in a very short time. They ran up debt in my name and manipulated their parents out of their retirement savings. I was then called upon to re-capitalize the operation, and my meeting with their parents brought the whole thing into clear focus. It was not a complete lose-lose situation, as I had taken my share of the losses for three years to offset my tax obligations, but it was time to walk away, and the easiest path was to sell my share of the business to them. A quick drawing up of papers and they owned the business for one dollar and all the debts that had accrued. Free at last; free at last! At least for the time being. This time, it only took three years to hit bottom. Was this venture a success? It depends upon your perspective. I had learned a lot in the first adventure into small business and had established myself with the banks and my suppliers. I had credit galore and good credibility. At this point, I should have begun to understand how important it was to judge people on their character, but my life was mostly about trust and any suspicions I had about people were promptly dismissed. What happened next is well worth the telling. I have this problem of not learning from previous lessons when it comes to people.

Another one of my employees was an interesting chap who had ideas of owning his own business. He was from a good family, had an extensive education, and was every-one's idea of a nice guy to know. He managed to convince me that he and I could partner up and buy a tavern and lounge that he would run and we could split the profits. My part was simply to finance the operation, and he would do the management job. On the surface, a can't miss deal. We found a place for sale, negotiated a deal, and we became the owners. Things looked well, and the place was packed two nights out of the week. Money poured in and somehow disappeared. Debt began to accumulate, and I was asked to step in and cover our losses. My bright young partner had a few issues and it had taken it's toll on the business. Drinking, womanizing and finally drugs became his life. He lasted six months and called it quits. We were through, and I was stuck with a business I had no interest in and wanted no part of. It took three years to finally find a buyer, and that had to be one of the biggest reliefs I had ever felt in my entire life. Is a pattern starting to form here? It should by now, as I had gone through three businesses in less than six years.

The big turnaround came with walking away from a disaster or two, and reentering the not for profit field. A neighboring county was seeking an economic develop-ment director, and I threw my hat in the ring. I came in second place on the list, and was called six months later and offered the job. It came with some obstacles, and one was traveling 75 miles each day to the position, and a like amount of miles back. I was so glad to escape the rat race I had placed myself in that the driving distance provided the therapy I desperately needed to heal from three bad experiences. It was a one year contract, as the government had given the county a grant to work at making jobs in a very poor, distressed area. Many parts of the Midwest mirror this county. With mostly farms, three small towns separated from each other by miles and all having the same problems. Middle Indiana is a beautiful part of the world, and I often enjoy the memories of the experience and the people I met there. I wasn't there a week and, when going to a little restaurant for breakfast, people would come to my table and sit and open a conversation. They knew who I was and why I was there. But, and this is the big one; it is very hard to make bricks without a good supply of straw to make the job easier, and that is often the stumbling block that ventures like this face. There was enough money for my salary, and the local Chamber of Commerce provided a secretary and an office. How do you take a rural county in the middle of nowhere and make it into a good place to live and work? The dream is to attract business and make good paying jobs. To do this, you need an educated workforce or at least a good supply of trainable, unskilled labor. We did have a major highway built to interstate standards, but that was hardly enough to attract larger companies. Instead, we needed to focus on smaller companies with ties to big cities that wanted to relocate. Taxes, regulations, and high wages are the enemies of small business. Our efforts brought a Michigan company to our county and did offer a few jobs. Neighboring communities did better at attracting business, but they had the advantage of population size and educated workforces. All the effort in the world was not going to change much of anything, and my board members finally accepted the fact. We had some interest, but community objections overrode their relocating to the county. I even saw the defeat of a badly needed senior housing project due to fears it would decrease property values of nearby residences. It was a brick wall that could not be scaled or torn down. On another level, it turned out to be an even better opportunity for me to expand my horizons. It seems they had a community college program going in the county, and they lacked an instructor to teach the small business class. As I recall, the class was called 'How to start or buy and run a small business'. This county of twenty thousand people is a collection of three small communities, and my board members were community leaders, so it was a natural for them to offer my services to the college. This turned out to be a one night a week class of four hours of instruction. I was handed the textbook on the day the classes were to start, and I had a couple hours to read the first few chapters. I had what was needed, as I had made so many presentations and speeches that it became second nature to me. My twenty or so students were a delight, and everything went exceedingly well. I gave them good grades, and their evaluations led the college to offer me a full time position in my home town of Terre Haute. For those in the know, community colleges do not pay as well as universities, and the pay scale offering was incredibly low for what was expected of an instructor. In addition to daily classes, there was the task of counseling students to stay in school, and that might require evenings in addition to class time. I had a few meetings with the faculty, and they were enthusiastic about my joining them. It was a chance to return to my home community, but the money was just not there to justify taking on still another career. Looking back, it could have been a new path that might prove rewarding. Was this still another missed opportunity? I could have finished my education and had a comfortable career well into retirement. In this case, money talks, and dreams walk. I still had family obligations, and the small income would not have satisfied all our needs. I will have to leave that up to someone else to decide if I made the right choice.

1986 and 1987 were enough to make a person wonder what life was all about, and a lot of time was spent trying to make sense of what had transpired. I was still in Terre Haute, Indiana, and I had a very nice home, children nearly grown up, much difficulty behind me, and time to reassess what went wrong. A lot has been said and written about the character of the people you choose to include in your life, but we are sometimes blinded to this reality and the necessity to carefully examine the consequences of making bad judgements when it comes to people. I failed to take this into account on three occasions. I have to wonder where I would be right now if I had chosen better people. At this point, it is meaningless to speculate on what the outcomes might have been.

Now, at fifty years old, what was one to do with the rest of their life? Would it be much easier to just take a job and do something different? What would that be, and how would one go about making that kind of transition after all this experience? I picked up a couple of self improvement books and took the time to study what had been presented. It turned out that this sort of approach was aimed at people looking to find their way, and not for people like me who had chased their dreams and saw them to fulfillment. The old idea of 'going home' kept rearing its ugly head. Why take on still another new venture when you could fall back on your experience and take a position and carry on with a previous career?

Here we go again! Why not go back to what you were doing when your life took a hard right turn? Why not go back into community organization and fundraising? Get out the old resume and do some serious updating. Lots to tell, and maybe it would strike a familiar cord with some organization out there in need of a go-getter. Back into the job market with United Way of America and watch what happens. I fancied myself as a problem solver, a Dirty Harry of sorts, in the business, and I had the credentials to back up the claim. With mergers, reorganizations, business startups and all, why not claim this advantage? Offers started to come in, and some travelling had to be done. Some had promise, while some were the same old pot full of problems. All required relocating. At this stage, I was ready for a change. Anything with promise would be considered. I really wanted to stay in the Midwest, as I had been to other parts of the country, and most did not have four seasons like the Midwest. My getaways were walking, hiking and cycling winter and summer. No; it would be the Midwest or nothing. Here again, we make choices, and we risk a lot of other options in the process.

Months passed, and the offers kept coming. One was from Iowa, and it was a fund looking for a director to replace a retiring one. It was a good match on the surface, but have you ever been to Iowa in the winter? On top of that, the pay for the amount of responsibility did not match up. There are so many things to consider when finding a position. It is not just the need for qualifications, but the idea of once again facing the relocation hassles is sometimes more than anyone is prepared to do. I had moved and travelled a lot at this point, and change was no longer a scary proposition. I then decided I would consider moving farther south. My thirty-one years up north were behind me, and I had no thoughts of moving back up there, even if I was offered a good job.

And then came the offer to come to Hopkinsville, Kentucky and accept a director's job that was vacant and needed a big boost to clean up a major mess. Oh, no! A Terre Haute all over again, and even a little worse. Regardless, I needed a job, and a challenge. It was time to get back in the saddle and clean up the mess and perhaps retire in a southern town and kick back. Same scenario. In debt, no growth, uncollected pledges, community disinterest and a board in name only. What was I thinking? Too many red flags and I failed to see any of them. I had done this before, and this was a smaller community, so how hard could it be? Not two weeks into the job and my one staff person decides she can't work for me. A local woman, a young mother and few office skills to offer. She had been assured by members of the board that they would see to it that she got a job, perhaps with one of their companies. A search was on for a replacement, and after countless interviews with people who could not fill out an application, let alone have no typing or computer skills, I finally hit pay dirt with a newcomer to the community who had married a local boy and had a lot of business experience and computer literacy. We began immediately to assess

the situation, only to discover that no billing had taken place for some time, that we had no bank balance to speak of, and we were in debt. We learned that people on the board had signed the loan agreements with the banks. Past time to put a campaign organization together and much to do to try to turn things around. We succeeded in raising more money with the first campaign, and that continued into the second year. By that time, my popularity had gone south with so many on the board that it was becoming untenable. At one point, word had gotten back to me that I was a low down, Yankee, carpet bagger! Hard as it is to believe, Kentucky does consider itself a part of the South, even though they never joined the Confederacy.

At near the end of the second campaign, I was summoned to a meeting of the board and told that they were unhappy with my performance and asked that I leave the directorship. It shocked some of the members as they were convinced that I had done the job they had all hoped for, for years. But the leadership had made up their minds about letting me go. I remained calm and professional. I accepted their proposal on its face. I reminded them that professionals were expected to serve for three to five years in a position. They had even anticipated that requirement, and there was talk of a written agreement to hold them harmless for discharging me. To top it off, they requested that I remain on to finish the campaign, and like a good soldier, I agreed. At the end of the year, I was let go, and that was that. I filed for unemployment and initially it was contested. The appeal judge moved in my favor, and I was granted the unemployment compensation. I immediately took steps to contact the national organization in hopes of finding another position. The letters of recommendation were for the most part favorable, but more than one female board member accused me of being sexist and resistant to change. In today's parlance, that would be described as 'toxic masculinity'. That proved to be a huge disadvantage when it came to interviews. The subject came up again in subsequent interviews and turned out to be impossible to overcome. No amount of explanation would change minds already made up.

I am known by some to be a resourceful person, and when all else fails, I draw upon my experience to fashion a new approach. I found myself in an awkward situation, as I had sold my home in Terre Haute months before and was renting a townhouse in my new community. I thank my stars my wife had found a job in her area of expertise as a bookkeeper, so we had an income to allow us to get by. Months passed and job opportunities dried up. I thought about sales, or real estate or even starting a new small business.

My other hobby comes to the rescue. Having been in the car hobby most of my adult life and using the hobby as therapy for the kinds of stress I had been under most of my working life, it seemed like a natural transition from the professional life I had been in for so long. I had a strong interest in cars and became quite good at restoring them and fixing what was wrong. My collection had followed me down to my new home, and had to be reduced to find enough space for all of them. At that point, I managed to find some property that fit the bill and moved my remaining cars into the new facility. I found myself with lots of time on my hands, and the hobby got a fresh start. I tinkered on the cars and actually started buying and collecting again. The problem was that all this effort did not provide any income. What to do? Well, why not go into the used car business? I had made many contacts through my job and with the hobby community, and it was a simple matter to learn the business side of the industry. I took a salesman job in a local new car dealership to hone my skills, and met a good number of people who were just like me in that they had ended careers, not by choice or by lack of job opportunities in their field. It looked like the over fifty age group that had been through some difficult times, and the car business was a handy alternative that could be a good income source. It turned out to be a real eye-opener, and all the horror stories that are spread around about the business were true. I 'made my bones' in about three months, and that became the springboard to a car lot of my own. It turns out that it takes very little to go into this business, money wise. You need a location, and you need a little start up capital to buy the beginnings of your inventory. A license to sell and a huge insurance policy form the basics of a dealership. If you stay small, you need no hired help, and sales people work on commission. I was able to hire a part time salesman, and he knew the community better than me. He was part of our large minority population, and everyone seemed to know him. He was not your average person, and really never held a steady job for long. He preferred to 'free-lance' and was quite good at it. He worked on commission, and we agreed to split any profits. That lasted for a few years, and we finally parted ways on good terms. I think he just got burned out and wanted to try something else. We remain friends to this day, and I see him once in a while downtown. He has tried a few more ventures and somehow manages to survive. I continued in the business, made a few dollars, added to my personal collection of cars and managed to pay the bills. My losses offset my wife's earnings, and we paid little or no taxes as a result.

After thirteen years in the business, I finally came to realize that it was pointless to continue. I was keeping the business going, but there were no substantial rewards to be had dealing in old cars and people with little money to spend on anything. It was time to face retirement once more and I had purchased a large building downtown and stored all my personal cars there. It was old and needed a lot of repairs. I worked at getting it weather-tight and remodeled the office, making it larger and re-doing a very old bathroom. I quickly got settled in, and had a nice place to go every day and tinker on my cars. I had internet and phone installed and spent a lot of time on the computer.

With all this time on my hands, I decided to chase another dream I had been putting off, and it had to do with a bedroom set that was available back in the 70's by an expensive furniture company called Ethan Allen that sold high end products. I had one of their catalogs from a long time back, and it had very good illustrations of what they offered. With that in hand, I set out to find a furniture maker who would make a replica of that design. As it turns out, that was not going to be easy, as most furniture is now made overseas and few shops remain that could handle such a project, even if they were inclined to do so. Most shops work on large orders, and to drop things and do a one of a kind is not how they are geared. I did get several apologies, but that would not get me what I wanted. I started looking for local talent who might take on the challenge. I was told about the local Amish and Mennonite families that did this sort of thing, and began the search with renewed enthusiasm. Again, no luck, as most craftsmen remained in Ohio and Pennsylvania, and there was no one local who had the time or interest in tackling such a job. And then, something amazing happened. Seems there was a local man who refinished and repaired antique furniture, and had a woodworking business running out of his attached garage. Once I found him, the whole thing started to take shape. Turns out, he was a retired Army sergeant with an attitude about most things, and especially people. He was stationed in Germany and took classes in wood carving, and discovered he was quite good at it. When he retired, he went back to college and got a degree in social work. He tried that for a time and found that it was not what he imagined it would be, and finally walked away from it. He turned his woodworking hobby into a small business and called himself the Wood Doctor. He had quite a few clients, and fixed and refinished antiques. If they needed reassembled and needed pieces replaced, he had the skills and equipment to do the job. I was impressed with his shop and just needed to get on his good side first. To say he was rough around the edges would be too charitable. He was coarse on most things, and as mentioned, with people. I had dealt with his kind and just knew that under that tough surface, there was a genuinely good soul. Once the ice was broken, we got down to business. Most of what I wanted, he could do, but when it came to turning the large posts, he was at his end. But we started with dimensions and design and came up with what I was after. I soon learned that there was a millwork shop in a neighboring town that had the equipment and the talent to tackle the rope-turned posts for the bed. It would take six or eight weeks to make the posts, and they would call me when they were ready. In the meanwhile, Peter and I would start on the backboard, or head of the bed. An elaborate piece that had to be made in two pieces in order to get it through standard doors and into a house. There would be eight hand-carved panels with linenfold effects and each turned out to take eight hours of carving to shape them. Then there were the matching panels in the night stands and the huge ten-drawer dresser. It took five months to complete the set. The local newspaper sent a writer and photographer to do a story on the bedroom set. My woodcarver friend got a lot of free publicity.

Now, I realize this is a side tale, but it brings out the point that if you want something in life, you have to pursue it. Some things cannot be simply bought or imagined into reality. It all starts with an idea, and then your drive and imagination needs to kick into high gear. Sadly, everyone is not filled with curiosity and the drive. Without it, most things will just remain a dream. Again, risk and change are strong non-motivators. If you can't overcome your fears of failure, you are not cut out for entrepreneurship. That part mentioned earlier about 'quiet desperation' is very real, and it infects countless lives of people who end up with regrets in their lives. You can easily spend your life in a dead end job, get the occasional raise and endure it. I know many people who worked the same job in the same company all their working lives. Not any longer. These days, a five year job is the norm. Things have changed rapidly.

Have I lived a charmed life? Not really; but without an imagination and lots of study, great teachers, the wisdom of truly brilliant people, and finally hard work, you can make something of yourself, help others, and have a great time doing it. There is no magic formula, and no two people are alike when it comes to leading a rewarding life. We start out a great deal alike, and then we start to grow into the person we become. The path is challenging and sometimes difficult, and many fall to the wayside with the first few disappointments. I believe you have to fail a few times in order to learn how to be successful. I think 'success' is an over-used word, and what one person thinks success is, has no bearing on what others think. You have to realize early on that you are your own person, and it does not matter one fig what others think. It is crazy to compare yourself to anyone else, as that is a big waste of time and a dead end path.

It is now January 1, 2022, and it took this long to get to this point. One might think the story is over, but there is much more to life than having several successful careers under your belt. You see, the trouble is, you can't do your main job and overlook what is happening around you. My specialty is/was community organization and fundraising. As such, my job, besides raising millions of dollars for charity, was to oversee the goings-on of the agencies we funded to insure that the moneys given went to the best and most efficient use. That is supposed to be a director's main function, and in larger United Ways, there are people that do this full time. In smaller communities, one has to wear several hats. You have to plan, organize, conduct, allocate and manage an office. Your staff is primarily volunteers, and you have to recruit the talent you need to get the job done. This calls for a widely diverse skill set, and many find their way out within just two years in the job. I have witnessed this scenario many times, and it is no fault of these well meaning people. The job pressure is very real, and that is just the tip of the proverbial iceberg. There is the politics of every organization that is part and parcel of the job. It is a lot like dancing and being extremely careful not to step on your partner's toes. Volunteer recruitment is the mountain to climb, it takes a lot of effort and persistence to achieve this goal. Once established, you have to give these top people a job and hold their interest in the work. This takes orientation, and praise and meaningful input on their part. Out there, in the campaign field, you have to establish relationships and keep them involved.

A side benefit of all this effort is the friends you make in the process. You find yourself in the midst of bankers, plant managers, social workers, directors and small and large business owners. I won't leave out the educators, as they play a large part in how communities function. Although you try your best to not get personally involved, it is bound to happen. Once you gain people's trust, they begin to see you differently and want to share parts of their life with you. There is a fine line between a working relationship and a friendship, and the real danger is crossing the line.

Ok, all of this is fine and good, and what happens next becomes an entirely different set of challenges. There is this aspect of sharing experiences with others and helping them sort out their lives, dreams and goals. It is called 'mentoring', and it involves taking the time out of your busy life to help someone grow up, gain confidence, try something new and pursue their dreams. I have done this on several occasions, and my usual subject is someone in their late twenties or early thirties. More often than not, they have an education, yet they are in jobs that are not even remotely related to what they studied. He was a music major, and he was a foreman in a steel mill. His father sent him to school and paid no attention to his choice of subject. It turns out, he was a music major. Years on, he wound up in his fathers' avocation, and with the degree, he was on a management track. He had gotten married, had one child and was purchasing a home. It looked like a pretty good living, but he was miserable. We had many long sessions, as he was loaned to me as an executive from his firm for a six-month period. He was impressed with the work I was doing as an executive in the fundraising field and thought this would be more to his liking. We agreed that he would have to go back to school in the evenings and get a masters in a totally different field. There was an offering in Public and Environmental affairs that would give him lots of options. He is no longer a foreman in a steel mill. The next project was to become a friend and a business partner, and now we don't speak. He was the spoiled child for my first venture into small business. With his father's money and my connections, we bought a going business. The end plan was to put his son in the business and make a permanent job from which he could not be fired. My partner was well educated with a degree in marketing from a large university in our town. What could possibly go wrong? In a word; everything. I was still directing a large fund, and this was to be a part-time venture where I would set the business up, and he would manage it. Three years in, and I was doing the buying, the books and dealing with the help, writing the checks and fixing the plumbing when I got off work. I would arrive home at midnight. I was given forty percent of the stock and a small salary. I told the father what was going on, and was asked to stay on until I was satisfied his son could handle the business. Have you ever had to deal with someone without a clue? I spent hours trying to show him the simple task of paying the suppliers, and he would get distracted with the bills and what we had bought. He just lacked focus. How did this end? I tried to buy them out, and that was not an option to his father. Then I tried to get them to buy out my forty percent of the corporation. We were doing three quarters of a million dollars a year at that point, and the buyout would be substantial. Here is where fairness and character come into play, and they proceeded, with the majority of the stock, to remove me as president. Time to lawyer up. Much time and money spent, and I finally just walked away. You don't win them all in the game of life, and you need to know when to stop trying.

The others come in the form of 'interns' that you are handed and your job is to train them to work in your field. The reward is you make friends for life by helping someone who needs some guidance and direction. It might take months, but in most cases it could take years. This area has now become a profession, and we call these folks job or career coaches. Could you do this full time with a list of clients? I don't think I could, as it is a serious drain on your time and your patience. This is not social work, but an opportunity to give back for all that life has given you. The rewards come from seeing someone succeed in their lives and the fact that you had a part in it.

Which leads us to another aspect of giving back. It is called 'lay counseling', and you don't need a social work degree to do this. You just need to be a good listener, have compassion, and try to stay objective and not get personally involved. Not easy work, but you can save and change lives. You only need to volunteer with some social agencies, and they will find things that you can do to help others. Churches are especially good places to start, as they have not only members but people in the community with no place to turn. A little time, some networking, and a few dollars will change lives for the better.

So, this is my story, and some must be wondering what it takes to be successful at what you are doing. There are tons of books out there describing what is necessary to find that 'perfect balance' in your life. Most will say a satisfying job, a family and hobbies or interests that you enjoy. Job comes in first, and if you are not happy with what you are doing, you need to think about making some hard decisions. The rest is going to be equally difficult to master. Having a family and children is a huge responsibility and should be your number one priority. This should come first, but it usually takes a poor second in so many lives. We see the dismantling of the family unit every day, and I don't think things are going to improve any time soon. But, the alternative for both men and women is to choose a single life, and not do the children route. A satisfying career is not a bad thing, and even marriage is not the answer for a lot of people. We are all individuals and it is up to each of us to choose our path. And, there is nothing wrong with making a few bad decisions and tripping and falling a time or two. It is very easy to say that if you don't do anything, you won't do anything wrong. My latest venture is an auto parts store, and it was a repeat of some of the others, in that the owner did not want to do it anymore. We agreed on a price, I gave him a substantial deposit and got a five-year payout at three percent for the balance that he would finance. No banks and no outside investors. Just an opportunity that came our way, and my son is running the place and we will soon see light at the end of the tunnel. My oft-repeated point is that you can fulfill your dreams, but it is up to you.

Now, for those that found this short tale interesting, you may wonder if this can still be done. The answer is a big, fat yes; it can. And now with the internet you can start and open a business without leaving your home. I am speaking of e-commerce, and that is the buying and selling on the internet to what could be a world-wide market. Many entrepreneurs have taken this route and have become successful. The market reached the multi-trillion dollar level just a few years ago, and it is growing. I dabbled in this and found it fun and profitable. When I still had my used car business, I also played with my hobby of vintage audio equipment. On slow days, I would search for these items on the internet, and mostly on Ebay. I would find items of interest, working or not, and fix them, or pay a technician. I would then put them back on Ebay and watch the bidding begin. Will it replace the 'mom and pop' hometown business? No, I don't believe so. Enter the human element into the equation. People love to shop and meet people and see what is out there close to home. There is this thing about looking, touching and holding things you find interesting. You can immediately picture yourself enjoying this item. Sometimes you find it hard to put it back down. Your impulse might kick in, and you just know you have to have it. It may be something you use all the time, a necessity, but it may be something decorative, or serve some function that you somehow overlooked. If you are artistic, can do amazing things with simple objects, or arrange flowers or sew quilts, you are on your way. Another area that is growing is service, and that can be done online. If you have skills repairing things, then your window to the consumer is a simple advertisement saying what you work on and can fix. From a pure economic standpoint, it is an opportunity to get in with very little capital and no need for a storefront to do business. I have always enjoyed the part about people starting a business on their kitchen table or in their garage. It has been done, and maybe you have an idea that can make that a reality.

I sincerely hope that what I have presented here will reach someone out there with a dream of becoming their own person; someone who is ready to take the one giant step in their lives and find some meaning and happiness that has escaped them up to this point. As I pointed out earlier on, only about one person in a hundred will actually take their idea and run with it. You could very well be that person, and you have to understand the risks before taking the first step. Life can be an adventure, or a dull journey. It is up to the individual to make the choice.

Isn't it strange
That princes and kings,
And clowns that caper
In sawdust rings,
And common people
Like you and me
Are builders for eternity?
Each is given a bag of tools,
A shapeless mass,
A book of rules;
And each must make-
Ere life is flown-
A stumbling block
Or a stepping stone.

— 'A BAG OF TOOLS' BY R. L. SHARPE

RISKS AND REWARDS

www.ingramcontent.com/pod-product-compliance
Lightning Source LLC
Chambersburg PA
CBHW051456140726
47987CB00006B/2744